TEMPS
CHANEL

© 2003 Assouline Publishing
601 West 26th Street, 18th floor
New York, NY 10001
USA
Tel: 212 989-6810 Fax: 212 647-0005
www.assouline.com

Translated from the French by Datasia

ISBN: 2 84323 511 1

Color separation: Gravor (Switzerland)
Printed by Grafiche Milani (Italy)

All rights reserved.
No part of this publication may be reproduced, stored in a retrieval system,
or transmitted in any form or by any means, electronic, mechanical,
photocopying, recording, or otherwise, without prior consent from the publisher.

GREGORY PONS

TEMPS
CHANEL

ASSOULINE

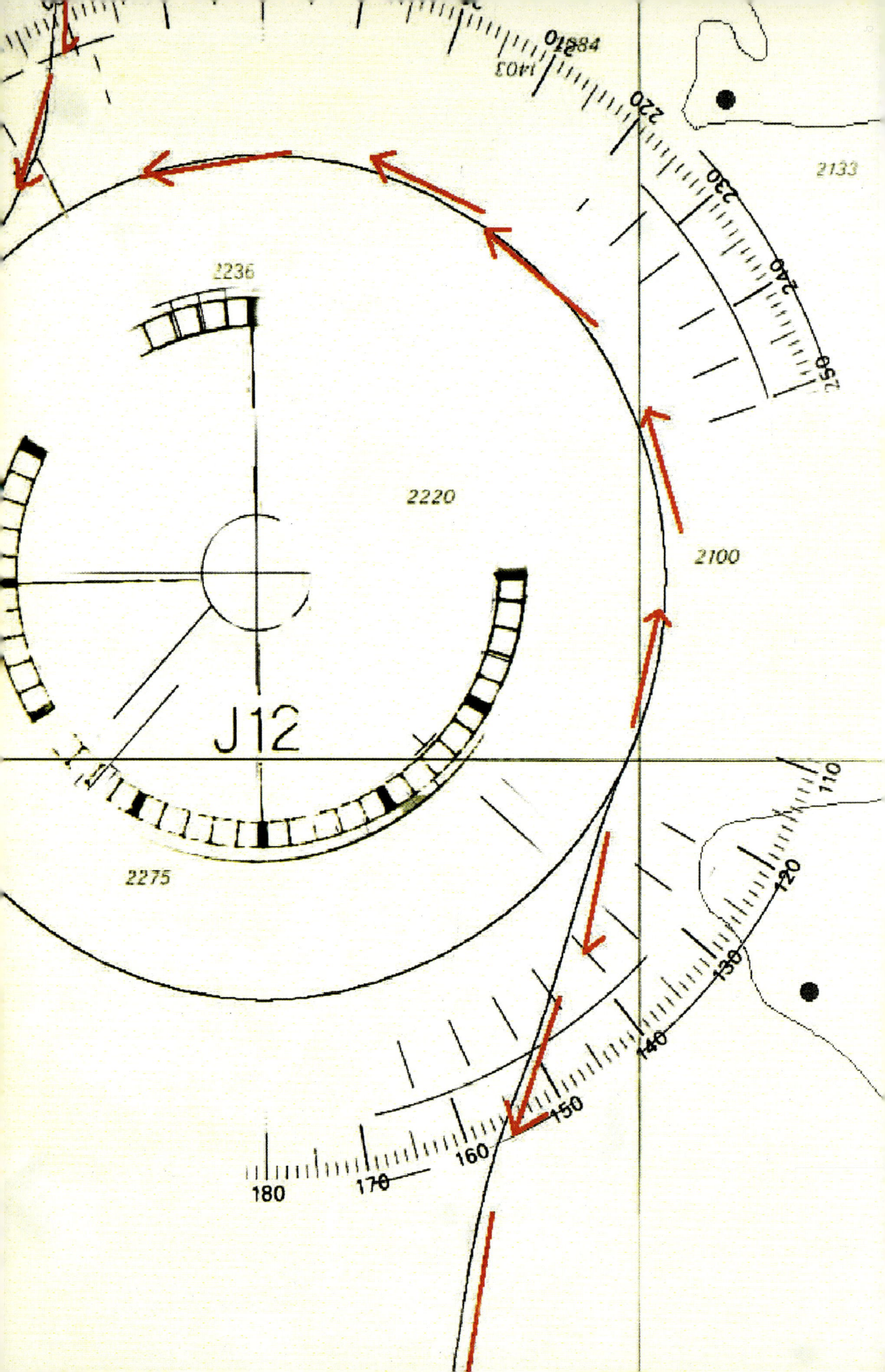

SUMMARY

CHEATING TIME	7
JACQUES HELLEU, THE EYE OF CHANEL	10
THE WATCH-MAKING CRADLE OF LA CHAUX-DE-FONDS	17
ABSOLUTE CONTRASTS	27
A FAITHFULNESS CODIFIED BY THE EPHEMERAL	57
THE PEARLS LIVE FROM LOVE	97
AN ELEGANT LIMPIDITY	111

CHEATING TIME

As she had no time to lose, Mademoiselle Chanel chose to take her time. Born at the end of the XIXth century, she quickly guessed that the century that was opening up at her feet, the twentieth, was there for the taking. She wanted to make it her time, to be involved in her period; she wanted to make her name and her language known. So, she took her time in conquering it, using her hands as her only weapons, taming materials with a look that was sharper than the scissors that cut into the habits of the past. Ambitious, she made outdated traditions look ridiculous. Generous, she freed women from their old-fashioned fetters. Triumphant, she created the "Chanel style", as one might speak of the Empire style. She remains one of the only creators of the century, if not the only one, that left her name to a garment and several accessories – the Chanel suit, the Chanel court shoe, the Chanel matelassé or quilted bag, the Chanel costume jewellery… *"Fashion goes out of fashion, style never"*, she never stopped saying.

It is often said that she had "the instinct of the moment", but in fact she spent her life fleeing and escaping from the past. Gabrielle Chanel fought constantly against time. Against her time, which she had to rid of prejudice, when women didn't dare to cut their hair, wear trousers or lay in the sun. Against the time that passes deteriorating the beauty of women, the morals of men and the harmony of the world. Against those years that betrayed friendships and erased references: in 1954, who would have wagered on the comeback of a seventy-one year old woman, still passionate for her career? Maybe this is from where her fascination for the hard-wearing and simplicity came, a pledge of eternity: *"She no longer imagined, wrote Edmonde Charles-Roux, that luxury could have another end other than to make simplicity natural."*

Often, on the balcony of her suite at the Ritz hotel where she lived, Mademoiselle Chanel admired the Place Vendôme, an unchanging stony defiance to the "progress" that had so often disfigured Paris. The photo is well known with opposite her, from the other side of the column, the building occupied today by Chanel, a disturbing veiled reference to history. The building – it's certainly striking – which was the headquarters of the Westminster Bank at the time, like the English Duke of the same name who was the most famous lover of Gabrielle Chanel…

She did not yet have the Place Vendôme in her sights when she launched her famous N° 5 perfume in 1921, but her lucidity led her to imagine the bottle stopper in the particular octagonal form of the square. A square shaped like the emeralds that Westminster gave her. Another coincidence. A familiar everyday form as demonstrated the gilded, faceted corner Spanish mirror placed in the entrance of her work apartment on the Rue Cambon. A form that can be found in the first watch that bore her name, the "Première" that was launched in 1987.

Young, Gabrielle Chanel didn't wear a watch. She lived her life and her time as she created them, in the most naïve contempt of appropriateness and common practices: the hours didn't have the same length for her as for those close to her, whom as a result sometimes suffered. She didn't like those little charm bracelet watches that were meant for women, calling them *"microbes"*, quoting a well-known mark. She later borrowed the watches of her lovers, just as she modified their suits or their sweaters. She already understood that the watch, a key object in the century of speed, should be solid, ordinary and fine. The post-war years confirmed her taste for large Swiss watches worn with white bracelets that she often offered to her friends. Is it really a coincidence that she first wanted to live in Switzerland, the world's cradle in watch making, when Paris no longer recognized her, before making Lausanne her last dwelling place?

Her adorable trickery with time and lesson in behaviour, *"By coquetry even the passage of time stops for a woman,"* right up to her ageless nickname of "Coco". The objects of Chanel remain, for the women who know how to listen to their desire, the subjects of pleasure and the symbols of luxury that are collected together by a rule of unchanging seduction. When Roland Barthes noted that, *"Fashion rests on an intense feeling of time; each year, it destroys that which it has come to love, it loves that which it will destroy"*, he underlined the peculiarity of Chanel. An exhausting struggle against time, a battle lost in her personal life – all finished by escaping from her, especially those who she loved – to be won in her historical destiny. Again Roland Barthes, *"Chanel made the very thing that kills fashion, the duration, into a precious quality."*

JACQUES HELLEU, THE EYE OF CHANEL

A vast white office, pure-lined furniture: dark and light. A huge, subtly off-centred black and white photo, and a single spot of colour, a work of art, whose remarkable blue extinguishes the blue of the sky. A silhouette all in black with just the touch of white of his hair and the blue of his eyes: Jacques Helleu, the artistic director of Chanel.

"I started out in the company at the age of eighteen at the request of Pierre Wertheimer, who asked me to take care of, 'The problems of taste', I didn't really understand what it was all about and I still ask myself today what this enigmatic mission corresponded to. In fact, after artistic studies and a hesitant vocation as a painter, I was somewhat looking around for which path to take in my life. In the beginning, Chanel allowed me to do a little bit of everything. I took care of the packaging then of communication and advertising in the 1960's. At the time luxury brands weren't used to developing communication. I had the chance to be involved in the saga of the Chanel 'égéries', of Suzy Parker to Estella Warren, with names as famous today as those of Catherine Deneuve, Candice Bergen, Ali McGraw or Carole Bouquet, to only quote a few amongst the thirty something of the most beautiful women in the world who have worked with Chanel, who demanded the best to photograph them: Richard Avedon, Helmut Newton or Patrick Demarchelier amongst others."

There are few files on the black slab of the desk, but an issue of Paris-Match from the end of the 1950's, a contemporary art revue, artwork for packaging and several coloured pencils.

"I could also mention the campaigns that we launched for the perfume. They confirm that, in communication as in our approach as watchmakers, Chanel has

Top
Jacques Helleu, Artistic Director of Chanel.

Page 6
Mademoiselle Chanel on the balcony of her apartment at the Ritz Hotel, in 1935.

Page 9
Chanel Watch and Fine Jewellery Boutique, 18 Place Vendôme.

Top
Drawing of a "J12" by Jacques Helleu.

always played independently. It was, for that matter, the spirit of Mademoiselle Chanel when she launched her collections: working intuitively, independently, with the only wish to fully express herself without holding anything back. The creation of Chanel was never due to such–and-such an advertising agency, some designer or another, but rather the contribution of outside talents – Ridley Scott, Roman Polanski, Jean-Paul Goude or Luc Besson – to our own identity codes, such as they have been formed by our history and by Gabrielle Chanel herself. It is this inner strength that has earned us numerous creation prizes…"

At the wrist of Jacques Helleu, a "J12" chronograph that he himself bought to life. It is well known that he has always loved watches and that he owns an interesting collection, amongst all the collections that he has assembled, ranging from ancient cars to electric trains. He has to be heard talking about his 1958 Facel Vega HK 500, restored like a piece of Haute Joaillerie. He has to be seen at the wheel of his 1957 Bentley Continental, of which there remains only one other example throughout the world. He has to be heard recalling his childhood memories, when he daydreamed in front of the workshop of the mechanic Cataneo at Saint-Cloud where the play-boy multimillionaire, Porfirio Rubirosa, had his Ferrari cars maintained.

"I have always felt a double interest for graphic perfection and mechanical perfection. The mechanic enthusiast that I am, whether about automobiles or locomotives, was the reason that drew me towards horology objects. Instead of my perfume bottles, I would dream about drawing Raymond Loewy's Pacific locomotive. Maybe I compensated with watches… There are delightful graphic expressions in the mechanic of a steam engine that I rediscover in the finest watch-making mechanisms. Success is spontaneously aesthetic, no doubt because it results more in a functional solution than in an artistic wish. In a watch I have always looked for this culmination of an idea that can only be found in timeless objects. Right from the conception of the 'Première' in 1987, I struggled to offer a strong model, a unique model, that would remain a reference and not just to launch a simple collection. The watch taught me throughout the years, to be even more rigorous and precise: a case or a bracelet is successfully managed to a hundredth, if not a thousandth of a millimetre. The force of a drawing is before everything a perfect answer to this double aesthetic and technical requirement."

It is well known that Mademoiselle Chanel liked to keep company with artists. She surrounded herself with the most original creators of her time. Various influences can be detected in her collections, but always in line with her time. The paintings of masters that covered the walls of the castles of the Duke of Westminster left her relatively indifferent, because her eye was that of a twentieth century woman. Jacques Helleu lives everyday in this contemporary universe, as he has chosen to live in a villa designed by Le Corbusier. Homage paid to the universe that has filled his aesthetic development.

"Reflections of avant-garde art from the first half of the XXth century are found in the codes of Chanel. The aesthetic shock that Malevitch left could only attract Mademoiselle Chanel whose taste was already for the black and white. The rigor of Le Corbusier can explain the ever rigorous and carefully crafted structure of her creations. It's this 'restrictive requirement' – the concern to always get to the minimum – that guided the conception of the Chanel watch collections, respecting the mark's reference points but with the impertinence that has always characterized the spirit of the company. It was logical to think of shaping the glass of the 'Première' line in the octagonal form of the N°5 bottle. The white square, black square rhythm held dear by Malevitch can be found in the 'Mademoiselle' watch, but it was necessary 'to invent' a masculine watch in a company with no former traditions in this subject. The 'J12' is a cocktail of influences and references ranging from the automobile universe (the black, the white numerals) to the high-tech (the ceramic, the jointed rubber links), passing by recollections of the America Cup. I have always followed with enthusiasm the America races, especially when the Baron Bich attempted the adventure with so much courage and determination on the boats designed by Mauric, the naval architect. I would go to see them in training on the Hyères Lake. The code name of their boats (the J classes of the America's Cup at the time, bought in the United States for team training) was… J12. The concept has remained in my memory, but I cannot exclude, for the codes of this 'J12', the memory of the last boat of Giovanni Agnelli. The 'Avvocato' had played with black, from the hull to the mast, passing by the sails and the dinghy. Black, the symbol of strength and energy!"

Black no doubt, but white too: the favourite colour (or rather colourless) of Le Corbusier, who only liked walls painted in white. White no doubt, but black always, because he had the hood of the cylinder head and the exhaust pipes of his Bentley painted in black gloss… Black like his Facel Vega, that he wanted blacker still by adding a touch of deep blue to the seventeen coats of the bodywork polish…

"But colour, the same as form, is only one of the codes to be respected in a watch-making approach. Beyond that, there is the idea, the technical detail that gives life to the product. Mademoiselle Chanel adored the quilting that can be found right up to the topstitched silk linings of her suits. How could this tradition be carried on, as yet never done in watch making? I thought about it without imaging that it could be done. It was one of our partners who found the technical solution: the 'Matelassée' was born from that collaboration. Then, how to keep and develop this tradition? Karl Lagerfeld proposed the material effects of chocolate bars in a fashion show. It was the right idea but still needed to be adapted for watch making. I wanted a watch as thin as possible that excluded a mechanical movement and an analogical watch. The technical solution came from Switzerland, where an original digital movement was developed: the numerals were in liquid crystal, themselves in a 'chocolate' style alphabet, inscribed in four squares. The new 'Chocolat' was conceived from this meeting between the idea and the industrial feasibility."

For him, the adventure is first of all on the inside. Daily strolls in the woods and tireless consumption of international magazines. A bath in current affaires through news magazines and regular visits to shows... home cinema, Jacques Helleu lives in a permanent bath of images, ideas and forms that guide his creation.

"Each season, its colours and its creative thoughts renewed. I am not the man of a workshop, but rather a solitary maverick, always a little apart from the routines of design professionals. What is better than 'l'air du temps', the current climate, to capture the idea that allows a watch to be imagined, the privileged instrument of the modern measure of time? I admit working according to my intuition, without computer, just with the simple assistance of a 'layout artist' who ensures the link with the team responsible for the prototypes. A simple photo is capable of giving me inspiration. The drawing follows, but the final idea is already there. My conviction is whole, already founded and I know perfectly what I want."

He is the eye of Chanel. The discreet, but intransigent, defender of technical quality for all he produces: Jacques Helleu instinctively knows how far Chanel can go to maintain its magic.

"The most difficult part is always how to convince the others of the validity of an idea. Seven years have been necessary to achieve the 'J12' such as we know it. Originally in 1994 the technical means of producing the watch, as I wanted it, did not exist. No one was capable of giving me the shiny and resistant black that I needed. The practical feasibility only came later with this ceramic nearly as hard as diamond. Moreover, no one saw the need for Chanel to meet a market for masculine watches... For the new 'Chocolat', a specific study was needed and a special electronic movement was produced, as it didn't already exist, to accompany the articulated slimness of our watch. One year of studies and trials has been necessary in the development of the digital numerals: four numerals stronger than two hands! It's no doubt long and atypical, but it is necessary in order to only offer watches that we are totally satisfied with. From the moment of conception, I already imagine the subsequent developments of the model that I draw, but the concept is there, already demanding in its logic and in its inner force. The concern of the commercial success never interferes with this creation: the success only compensates the totality of a rigorous process. We don't experiment: we have our convictions. The amateurs – male and female – appreciate them enough to incite us to persevere."

THE WATCH-MAKING CRADLE OF LA CHAUX-DE-FONDS

The craftsmen of the "watch-making valleys" have given Switzerland its reputation established since three centuries. At the centre of this Watch Valley, a real Silicon Valley of European watch-making, La Chaux-de-Fonds lives according to the watch. The scenery changes with the seasons – snow covered hills during the harsh winters from the Jura or postcard summer pastures – but the workshops remain. They are dedicated to a difficult art: the design and production of the most famous watches in the world. It is there that Chanel, between the prairies and pine trees, create their watches in their new workshops of 8,000 meters squared. The creative spark is transformed into innovative products thanks to the latest digital tools, combined with traditional watch-making savoir-faire, that ensures the totality of the operations, from the production of the cases and bracelets to the casing of the movements developed and produced by specialized Swiss companies. The integration of all of these operations into one site allows Chanel a strict quality control right throughout the production chain. Here, the Chanel time has already got ahead of itself.

Top
Bezel polishing.

Opposite
Dial setting.

Pages 16 ; 18 and 19
Hand setting on a "J12" dial ;
Chanel watch-making workshops at La Chaux-de-Fonds in Switzerland.

Pages 22 and 23
Quality control.

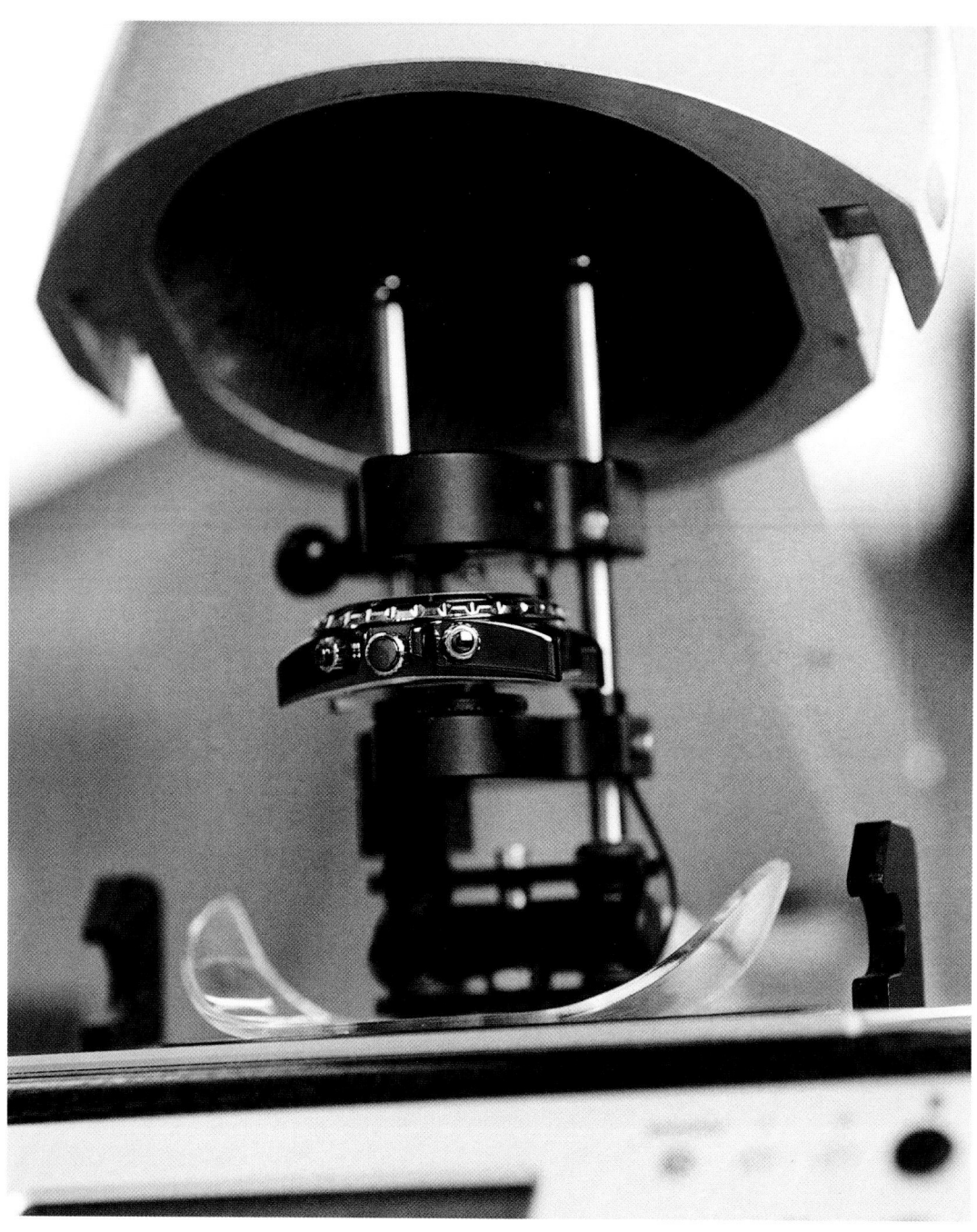

Top
Sapphire crystal glass setting.

Opposite
Bracelet assembling.

ABSOLUTE CONTRASTS

At Mademoiselle Chanel's, at number 31 of the Rue Cambon, the Coromandel lacquered folding screens at the wall: black and gold. The dress that she dared for women, so sumptuous in its simplicity that nothing stronger has been found in eight decades: black. The first bag that she created: black. The onyx of her favourite rings: black. The stopper of her first perfume: black…

The camellia, her favourite flower: white. The pearls at the throat of the women that she dresses and undresses at her will: white. The shirt that she borrowed from her men: white. The platinum that was her favourite metal: white. The bracelet of the watches that she was so fond of towards the end of her life: white. Malevitch's most famous and most "deconstructing" square: white on a white background…

The real sense that Gabrielle Chanel gives to luxury: black and white, like the black letters of her name on the white box of her N° 5 perfume. The signs of belonging that she has sowed on her way: black and white. Mutual reflection of inversed but completely complementary values: *"I have said that black compromises everything. So does white. They possess absolute beauty, the perfect agreement."*

Black, the "J12" sculpted in the ceramic of a deep black never before seen in watch making. White, the numerals inspired from the counters in a Ferrari of the best era. White, the new "J12", the first sports watch entirely made in a whiter-than-white ceramic of a northern intensity. Black, the numerals of the dial. The "Mademoiselle" watches all lacquered black and white, with white and black varnished bracelets. Dressed in black light, the new "Chocolat" in ceramic.

Because she loved the perfect agreements that defied time, Mademoiselle Chanel would have loved the black diamonds, these new symbols of luxury at all hours. She herself, always stretched between two poles, alone faced with time, "sensualized" the absolute by restoring a dynamic of life to the eternal confrontation of positive and negative.

CHA

J

AUTO

CERTIFIED CH

Top
Source of inspiration.

Opposite
"J12", water-resistant to 200 m.

Pages 28 and 29
Close-up of the "J12" Chronograph dial.

Pages 32 and 33
High-tech profile.

Top
Detail of an engine.

Opposite
Detail of the automatic "J12" Chronograph movement, certified COSC (Official Swiss Chronometer Control).

Pages 36 and 37
Black and White.

Pages 38 and 39
"J12" in high-tech white ceramic, 38 mm.

Pages 40 and 41
"J12" bezel in high-tech ceramic and tungsten carbide.

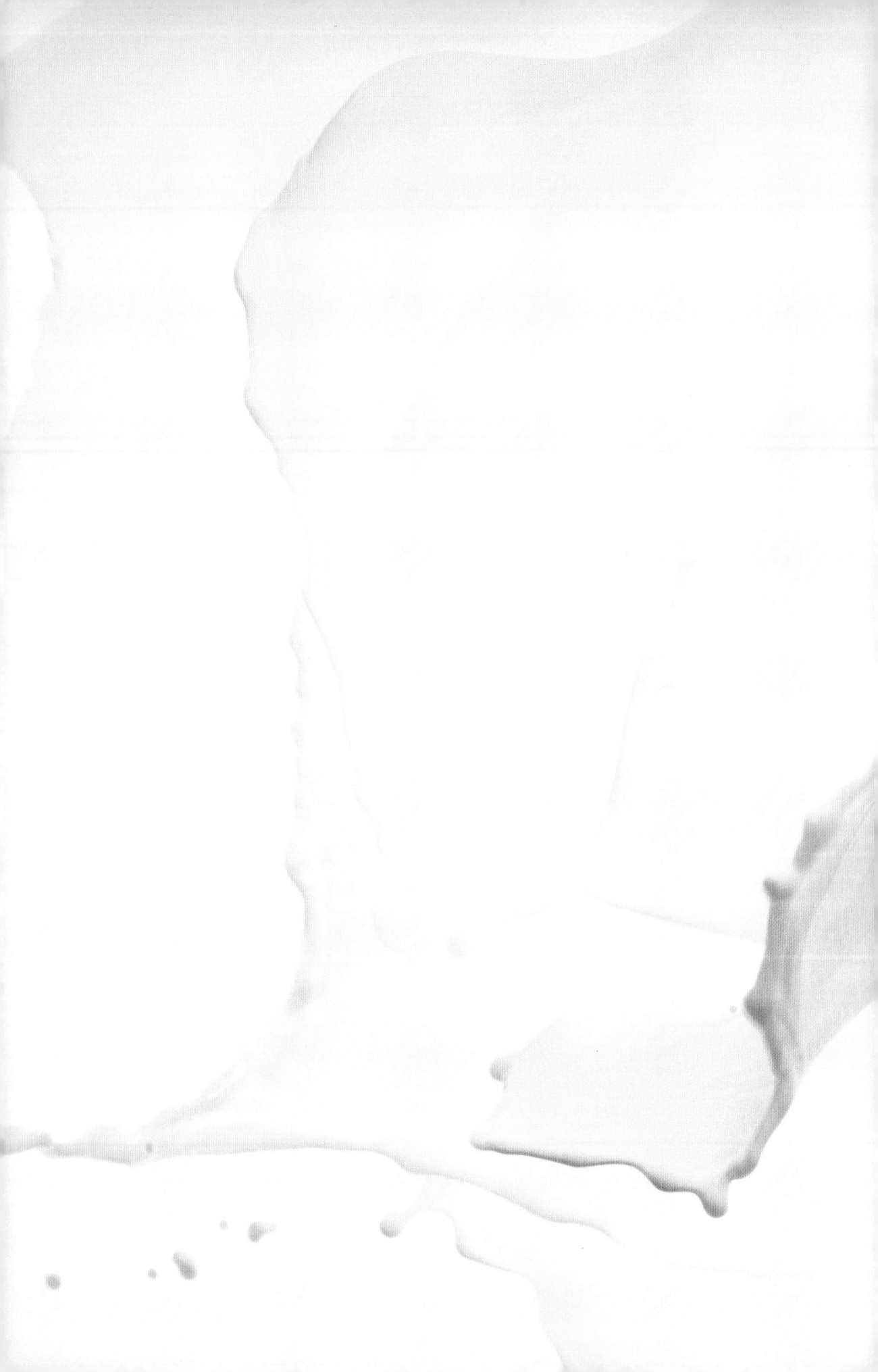

Top
Bow of a black yacht.

Opposite
Visual publicity of the "J12", 38 mm.

Pages 44 and 45
"J12" in high-tech white ceramic, 38 mm.

Top
White sail.

Opposite
"J12" in high-tech white ceramic and diamonds, 38 mm.

Pages 48 and 49
Rain of diamonds on the "J12".

Pages 50 and 51
"J12" white diamonds or black diamonds.

Pages 52 and 53
Positive/Negative of the "J12" diamonds.

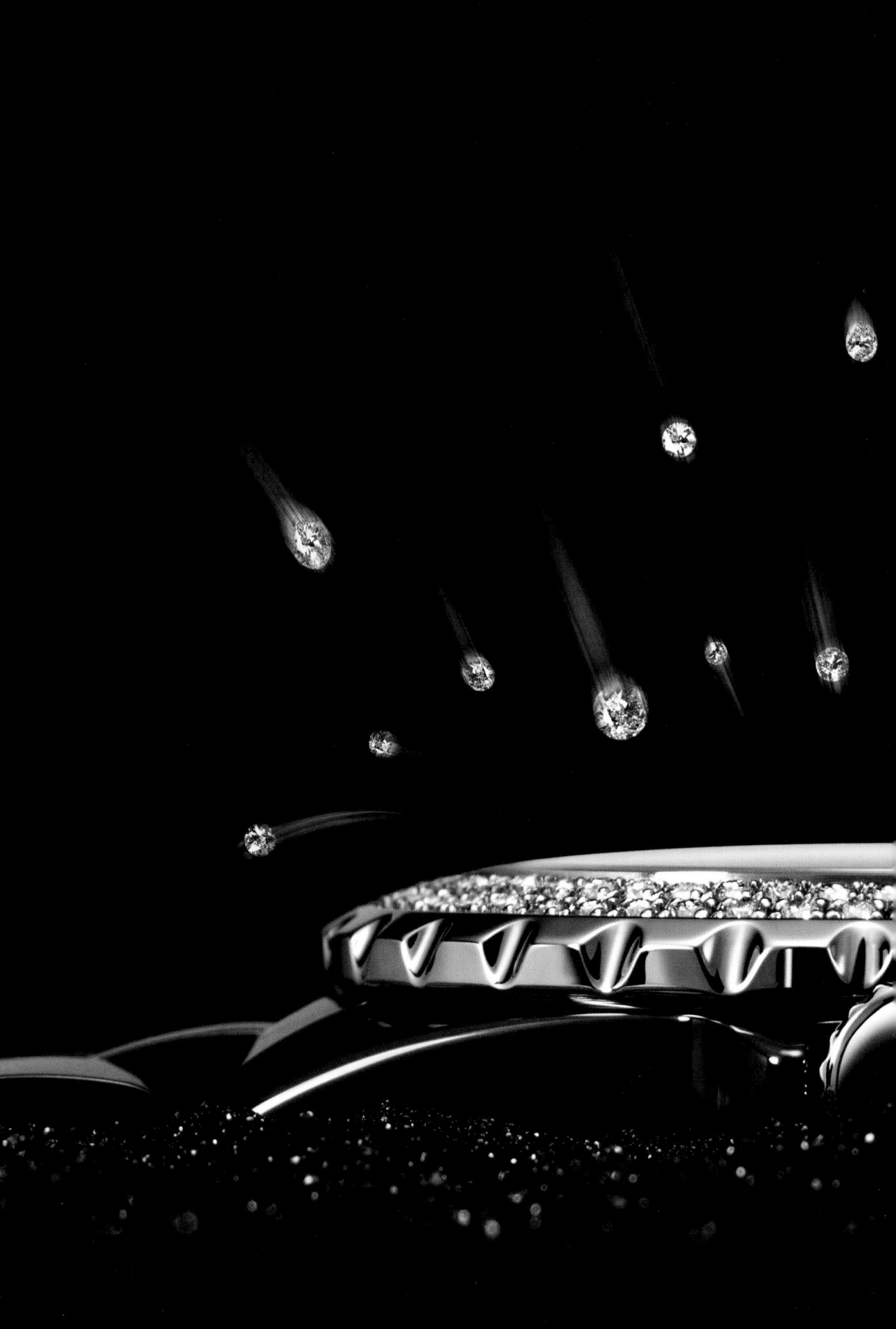

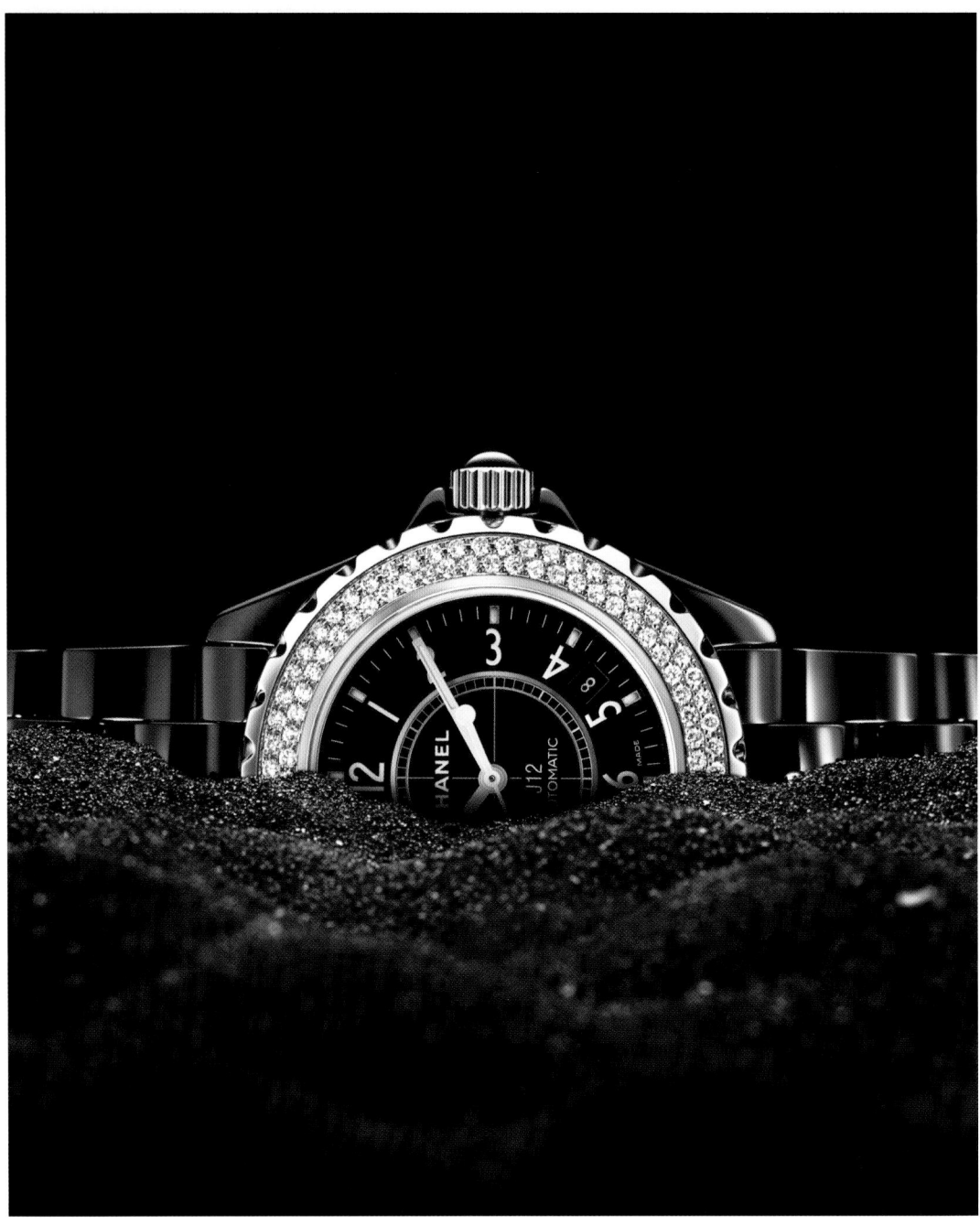

Top
"J12", white diamonds.

Opposite
"J12", black diamonds.

A FAITHFULNESS CODIFIED BY THE EPHEMERAL

"What's new? Chanel!" In 1954, practically half a century after her first milliner creations, Mademoiselle Chanel still caused a sensation in *Elle* who discovered her latest collection. In spite of the century's upheavals, the coherence of the message is intact; such the leading ideas of Gabrielle Chanel were strongly structured right from the beginning. Ideas that afterwards influenced the entire fashion universe. As Cecil Beaton wrote, *"The flowers that she has grown return each season, barely concealed behind the vague alterations that lesser talented couturiers subject them to".*

All her life she has made use of the same identification semantics: a suit with flowing jacket inspired from a cardigan that she wore in the 1910's, wrap-around skirts, a smock, fluid blouses, court shoes that slimmed down the foot without hurting, flowing strings of pearls. The basic elements of the Chanel style – or the "Chanel codes" as they are often known - picking up the main lines of her collections: *"I have created the most well known style in the world."*

The reference points of the gilded buttons and the costume jewellery. Her taste for geometry, like the faceted corners of the "Vendôme form" that is found in her bottle of N° 5 as in the "Première" watch. The chain and the chain bracelet, originally designed for Greta Garbo, and still joyfully used in belts, jewellery, bag straps and watch bracelets, in addition to the brass chain that "weights" the hem of the suits. The famous "little black dress". The long shoulder strap intertwined with leather, imagined so as to free the hands of women in search of social independence before inspiring the bracelet watch. The pouch style handbag, promoted as a piece of the obligatory uniform for the contemporaries. The quilting, inspired by the jackets of the jockeys from Chantilly, available in clothing and in bags, giving rise to different accessory lines, right up to the "Matelassée" watch, of which the "Chocolat" is the latest development. Her taste for pearls. Her passion for black and white…

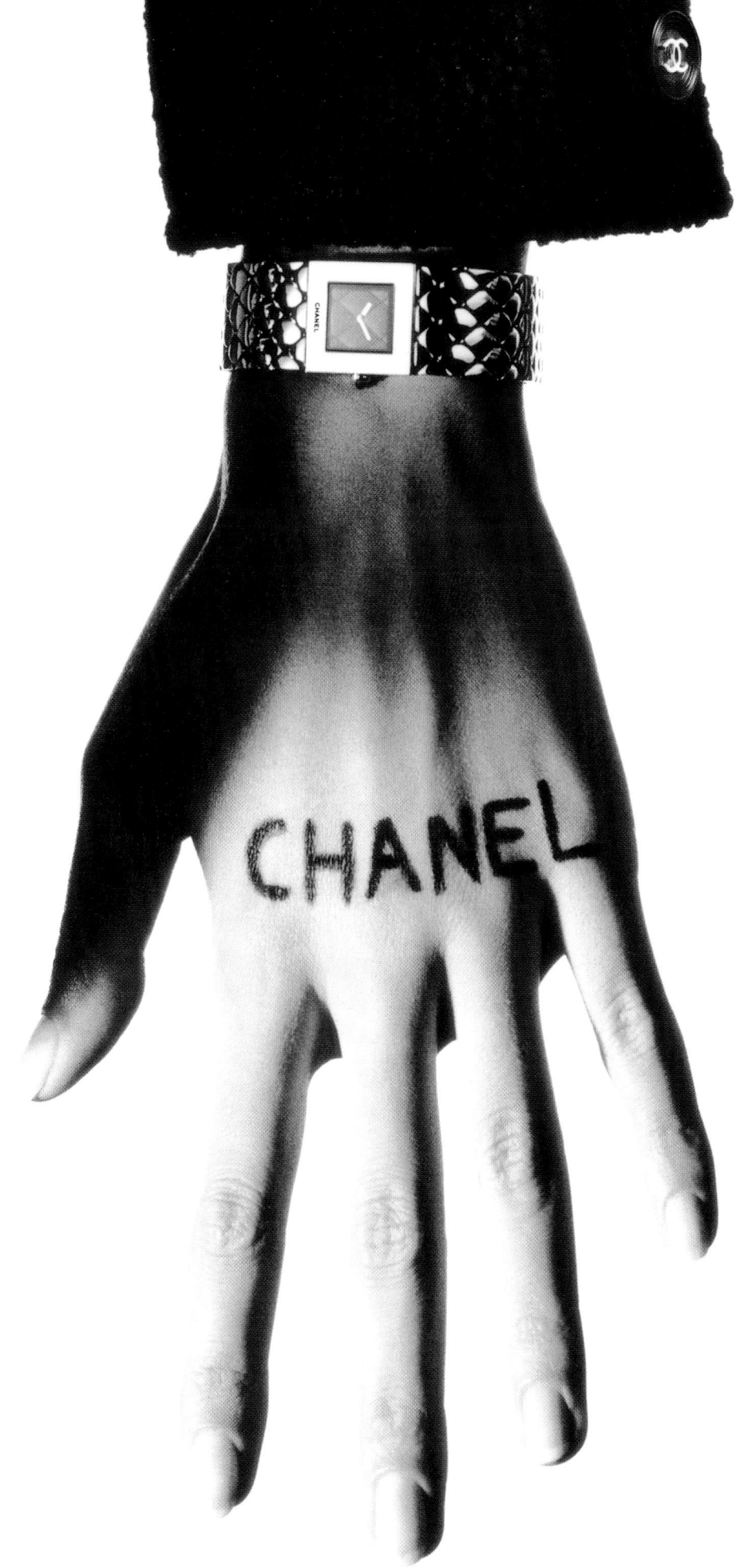

Top
"Matelassée" watch in stainless steel.

Opposite
Detail of the stainless steel "matelassé".

Pages 58 and 59
Image from the "Matelassée" press kit in 1993.

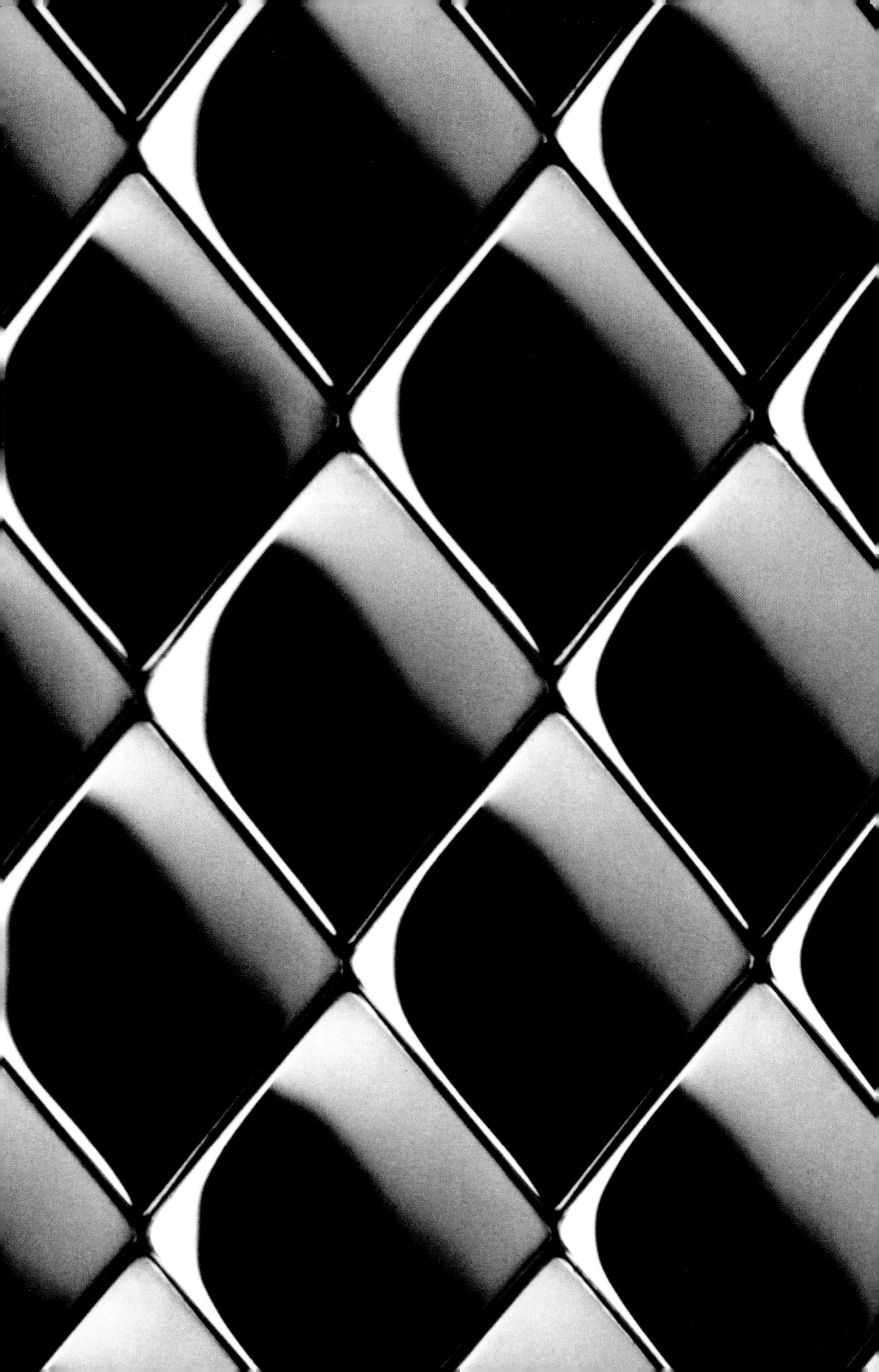

Top
"Matelassée" watch in 18-karat yellow gold.

Opposite
Detail of the two-tone "matelassé".

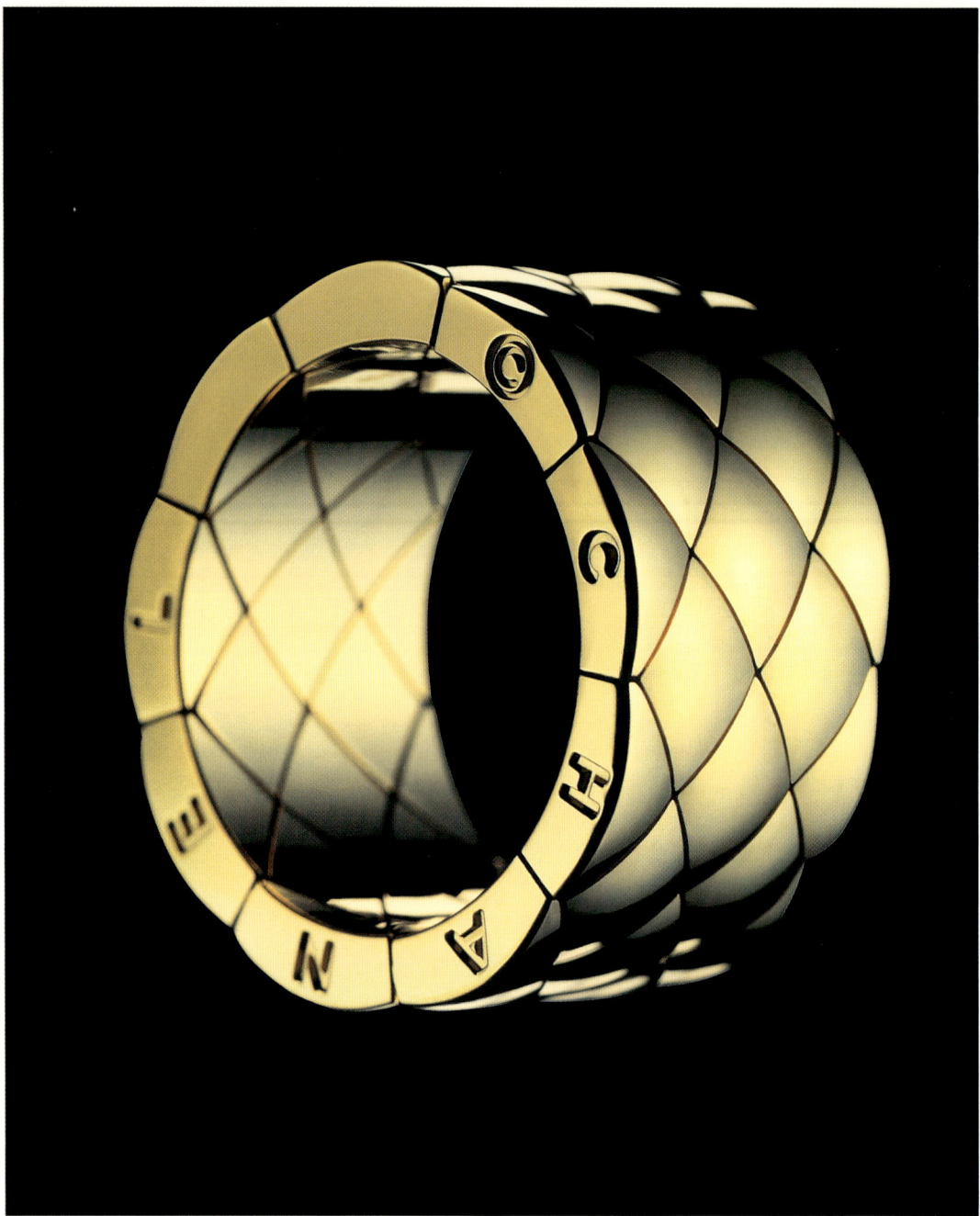

Top
"Matelassée Souple" ring in 18-karat yellow gold.

Opposite
Bracelet flexibility of the "Matelassée" watch in 18-karat yellow gold.

Pages 66 and 67
Chanel "matelassé" to infinity.

Top
"Ultra noir" necklace in 18-karat yellow gold and high-tech ceramic.

Opposite
"Chocolat" watch in 18-karat yellow gold.

Opposite
Drawing of the "Chocolat" watch in high-tech ceramic.

Pages 72 and 73
"Chocolat" watch in high-tech ceramic. "Chocolat" watch in stainless steel.

Pages 74 and 75
The art of digital.

Page 76
The famous N°5.

Page 77
"Chocolat" watch in 18-karat white gold, set with two rows of diamonds.

Pages 78 and 79
"Chocolat" watch in 18-karat yellow gold.
"Chocolat" watch in high-tech ceramic.

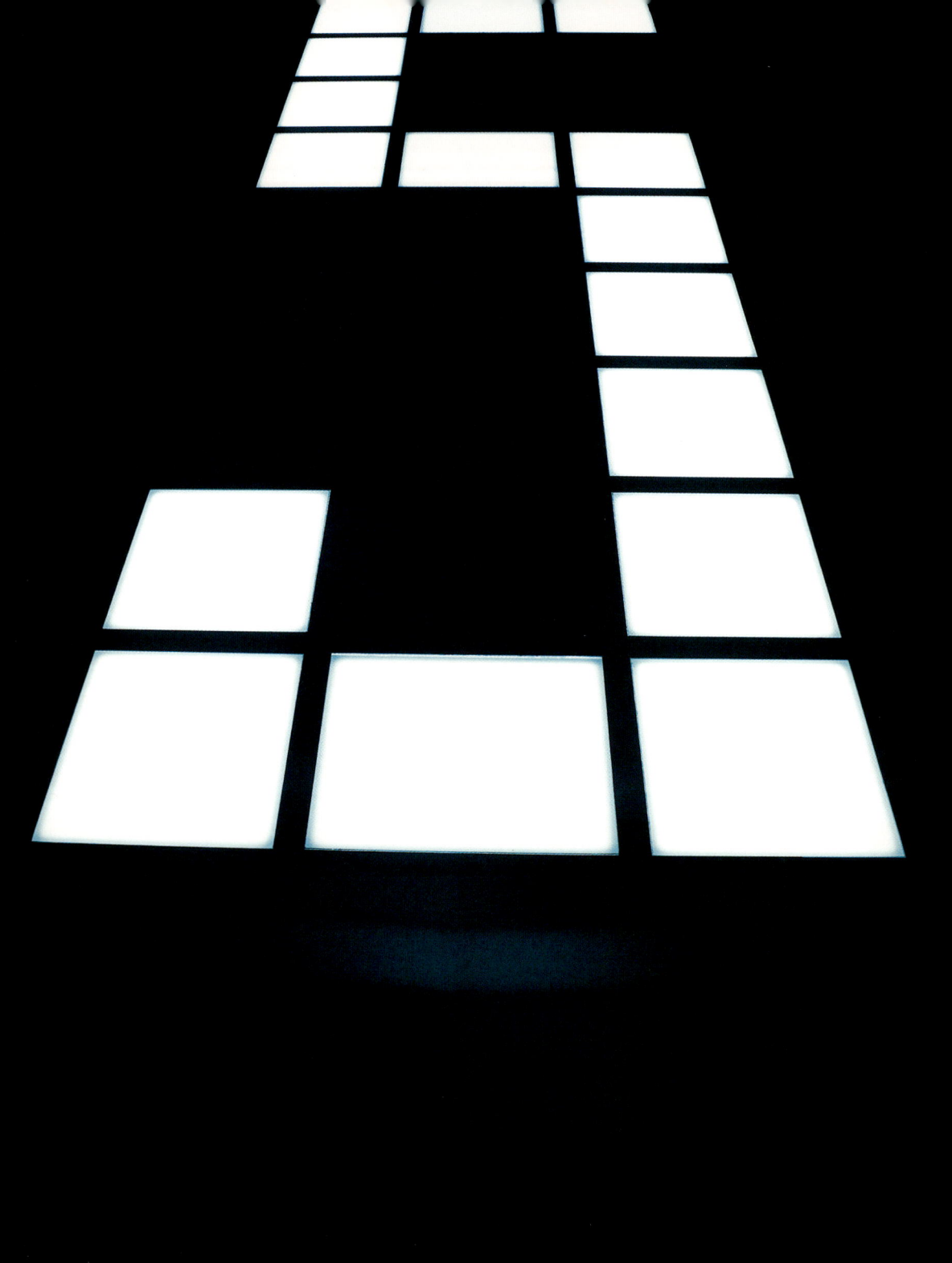

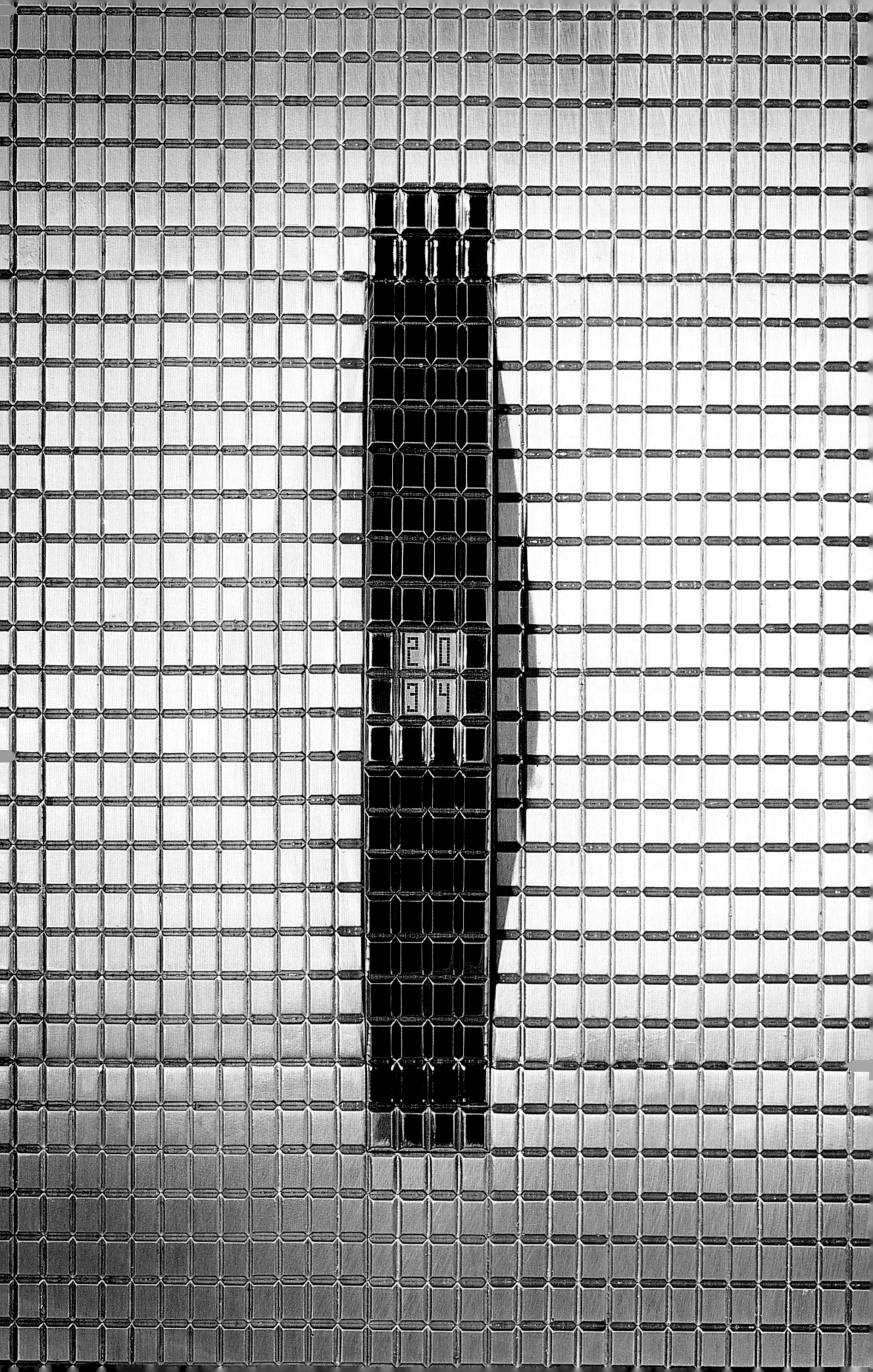

Opposite
"Chocolat" watch in stainless steel.

Page 82
Black geometry.

Page 83
"Mademoiselle" watch in 18-karat white gold and baguette-cut diamonds.

Top
"Mademoiselle" watch, white or black patent leather.

Opposite
Picture from the press kit "Mademoiselle, White and Black".

Pages 86 and 87
"Mademoiselle" watch, white dial on a satin finish stainless steel bracelet, or "Mademoiselle" watch, black dial on a mirror-polished, stainless steel bracelet.

Page 88
Aerial view of the Place Vendôme.

Page 89
"Première" watch in stainless steel interwoven with leather.

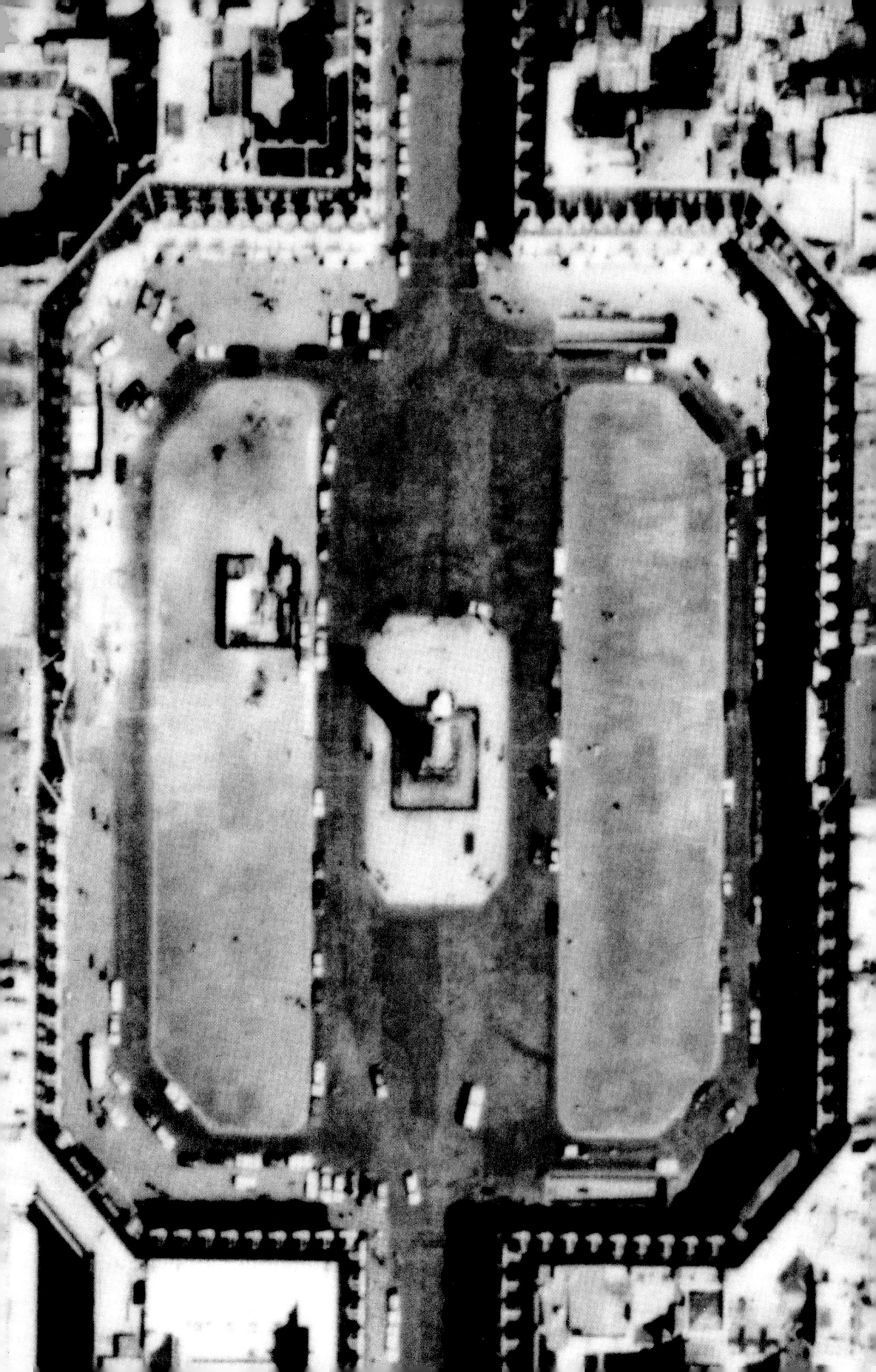

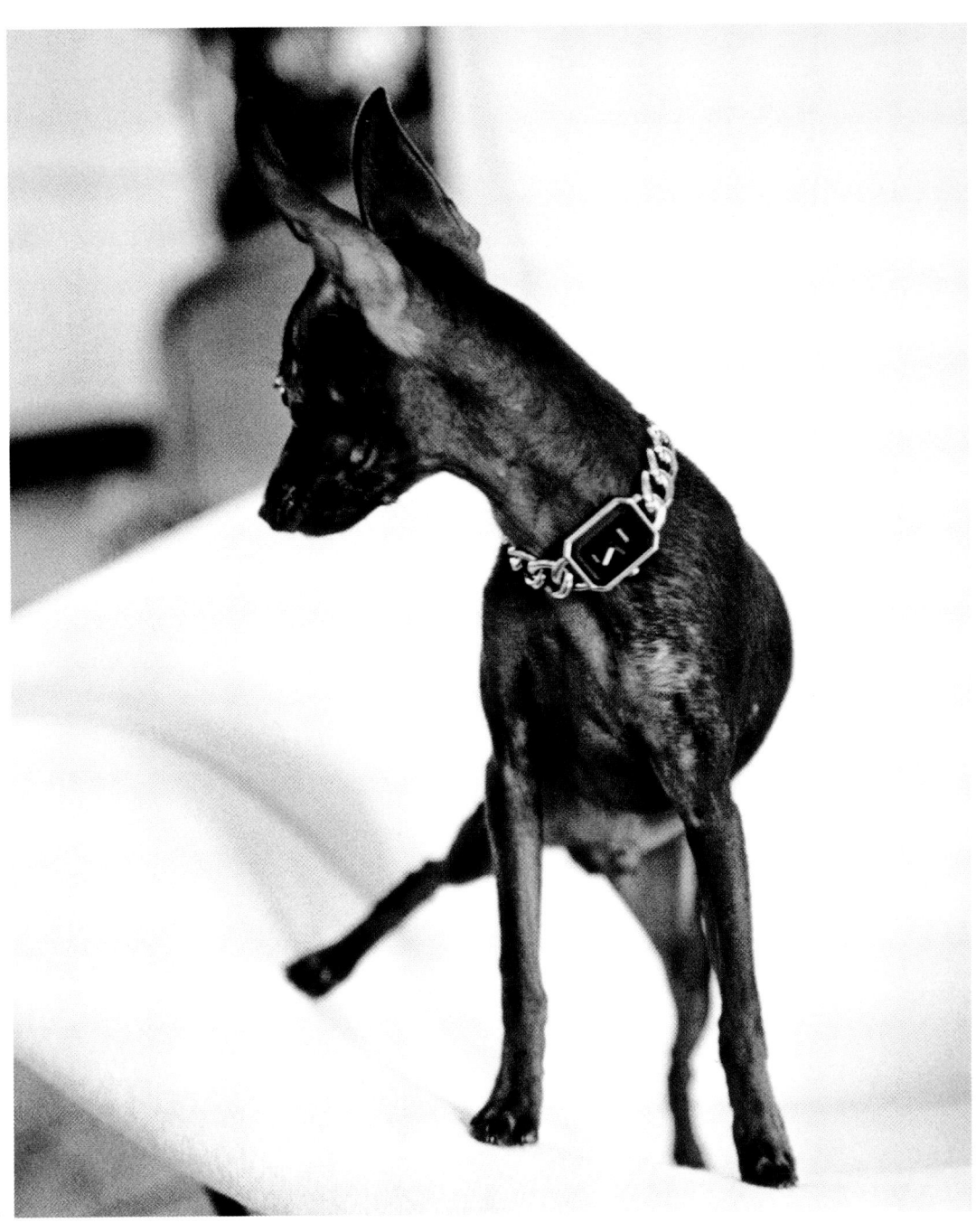

Top
Anecdote !

Opposite
Clasp detail of the platinum "Première" watch.

Opposite
Stainless steel chain bracelet "Première" watch, on Paul Morand's book "L'Allure de Chanel",
Karl Lagerfeld drawing.

Pages 94 and 95
Stainless steel chain bracelet "Première" watch, mother-of-pearl dial.

THE PEARLS LIVE FROM LOVE

Chanel and pearls? First of all a link with the sea, near which Mademoiselle Chanel had always wanted so much to live. An obvious link: Deauville, Biarritz, Venice, La Pausa, her villa in Cap-Martin, her taste for sweaters, the buttons of her suits, gilded like those of the officers on the yachts of her friend Westminster… Then the patience of a genesis, the beauty of the form and the secrets of perfection. A perfection born from the mysteries of a wound, the rareness of a discreet luxury, the apparent fragility of the extreme simplicity. Every pearl is a world because every pearl is living: it reacts to the person that accepts it and even to the love that is given to it. Neglected, it dies and loses its moonlike brilliance. *"A woman who is not loved is a woman lost"*, said Mademoiselle Chanel, a pearl too. It is said that they are luminescent under certain lights. Particularity of the sensual jewel originating from the sea to take its place and beauty on the skin of women.

The homage paid by Christian Dior, *"With a black sweater and ten rows of pearls, she has revolutionized fashion."* Mademoiselle Chanel liked to touch them and let their sheen fall in cascade: in a string around the neck just as in earrings or on a chain, she dared wear pearls with a sweater and trousers just as much as with evening dress. She kept them in the jewellery cases placed on the table in her lounge, mixing real pearls and glass beads without hesitation, treasures and illusions, junk and jewellery. She alone knew the authenticity when she attached them around her neck and wrists. She appreciated the immediate sensitive evidence, that of a natural work of art, magical child of sea life and mineral eternity, as the pearl has no need, as with precious stones, to be re-cut to bring out its beauty. Gabrielle Chanel would have loved the idea of using them for watch bracelets, jewels precious and functional at the same time because perfectly flexible and articulated. In these pearls there is a simplicity in the form and a guarantee of taste that challenges the time deduced by the watch.

Top
"Lumière" necklace in 18-karat white gold, South Sea pearls and diamonds.

Opposite
"Mademoiselle" watch in 18-karat yellow gold, cultured pearl bracelet.

Pages 100 and 101
Mademoiselle Chanel, by Cecil Beaton.

Top
"Matelassée Pearls" cuff bracelet in 18-karat yellow gold, cultured pearls and diamonds.

Opposite
"Mademoiselle" watch in 18-karat yellow gold, cultured pearl bracelet.

Top
"Mademoiselle" watch in 18-karat yellow gold, cultured pearl bracelet.

Opposite
Detail of the raw materials used in the "Camélia Secret" watch.

Top
"Camélia" brooch in 18-karat white gold, South Sea pearl and diamonds.

Opposite
"Camélia Secret" watch in 18-karat white gold, cultured pearls and diamonds.

Top
"Camélia Secret" watch in 18-karat white gold, cultured pearls, diamonds and rubies.

Opposite
"Camélia Secret" watch in 18-karat white gold, cultured pearls, diamonds and rubies.

AN ELEGANT LIMPIDITY

The two crystalline forms of carbon: the commonplace graphite that is used in our pencil leads, and the diamond. No substantial difference between the two, if not that the second has had a "hard upbringing", by the phenomenal pressures under the earth's crust, billions of years ago. Fascinating testimonies of authenticity. The extreme brutality of its birth gives the diamond an unequalled hardness. The extreme rarity of these beautiful crystals gives them a value just as unequalled: three thousand times the price of gold for this "coal dust"! Magic of the myth…

Enthusiast of simplicity, Mademoiselle Chanel was made famous by her costume jewellery. But how could she have, with her "taste for all that shines", not loved the diamond, a supreme symbol of purity, simplicity and inner strength? *"For all things, an instinctive desire of authenticity springs up, restoring an amusing piece of costume jewellery to its true value"*, she explained whilst presenting Chanel's first jewellery collection, "Bijoux de Diamants", in 1932. The minimalist casualness that she exhibits for magnificent diamonds finds an echo in the watches set with diamonds that Chanel propose today. In their golden rails, the diamonds accompany each movement of the wrist with their lightening. They are not there to decorate but rather to seduce. If they express luxury, it is by their rigor and their distinction more than by their demonstrative value. These diamonds live with their time: powerful and luminous, they modernize eternity.

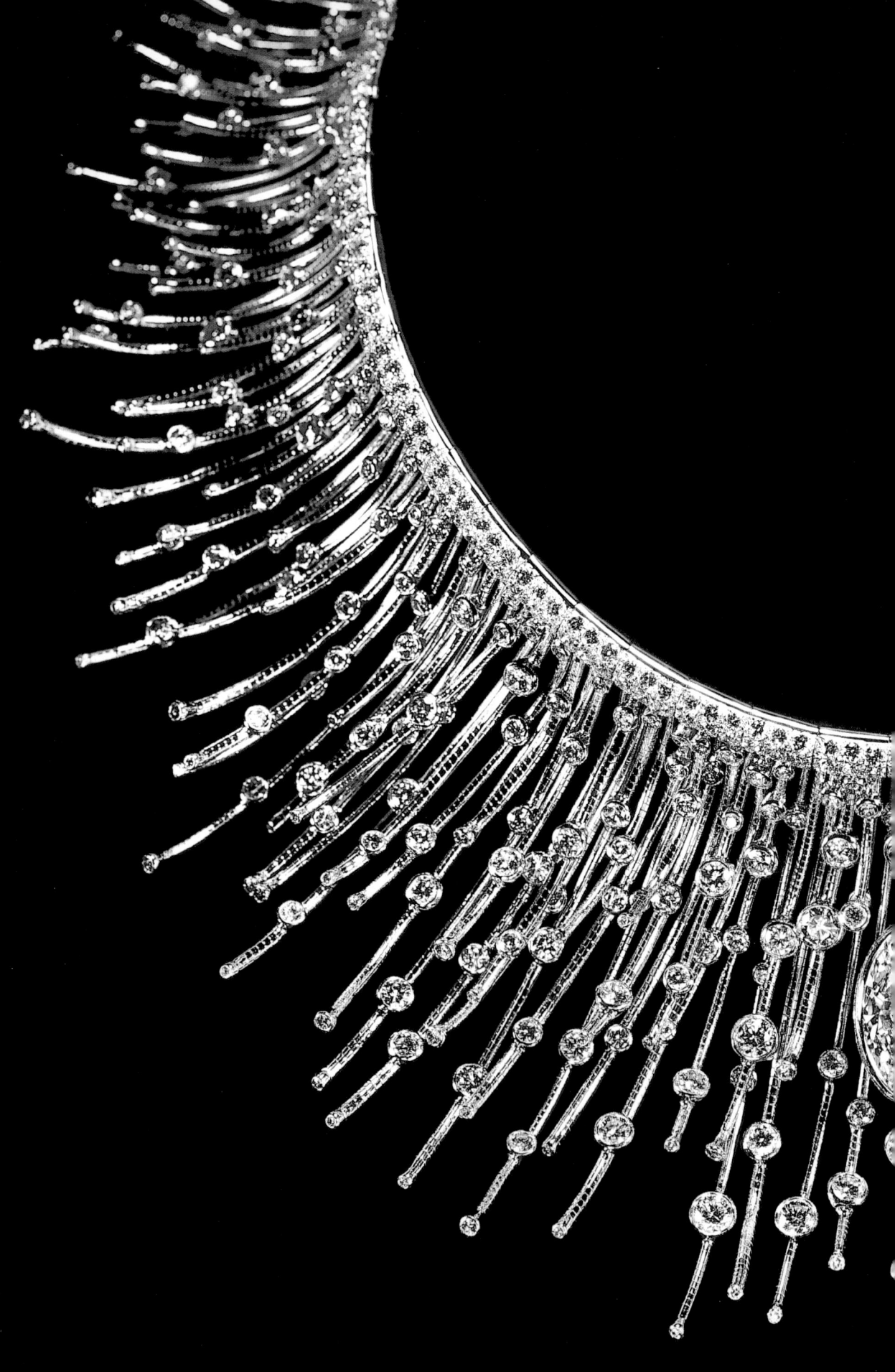

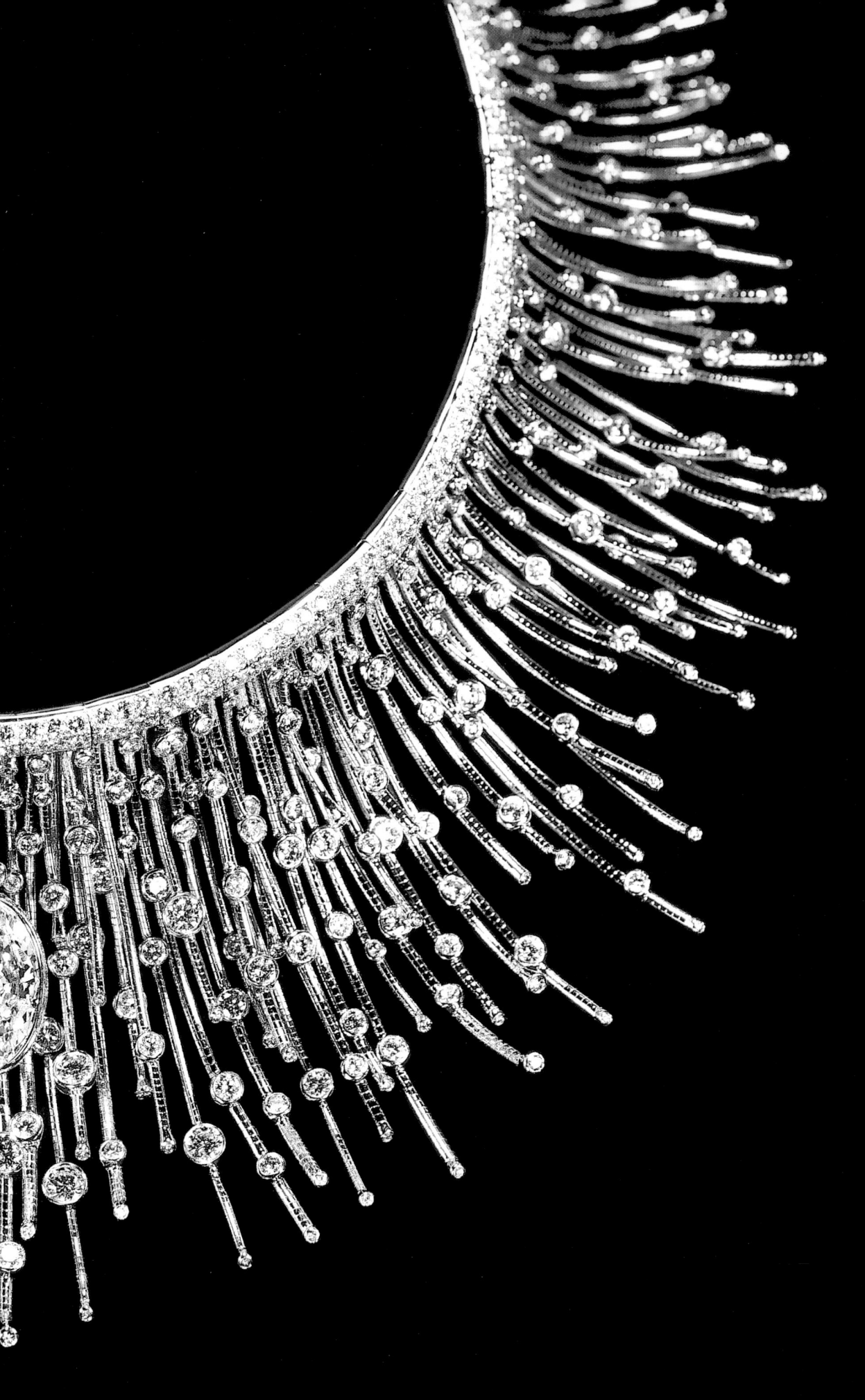

Top
"Comète" watch in 18-karat white gold and diamonds on grosgrain bracelet.

Opposite
Re-edition of the "Comète" necklace, created by Mademoiselle Chanel in 1932.

Pages 112 and 113
"Swing" necklace in 18-karat white gold, composed of 954 diamonds for a total weight of 39 carats and a central oval diamond of 7.50 carats.

Top
Re-edition of the "Comète" brooch created by Mademoiselle Chanel in 1932.

Opposite
"Comète Secret" watch in 18-karat white gold and diamonds.

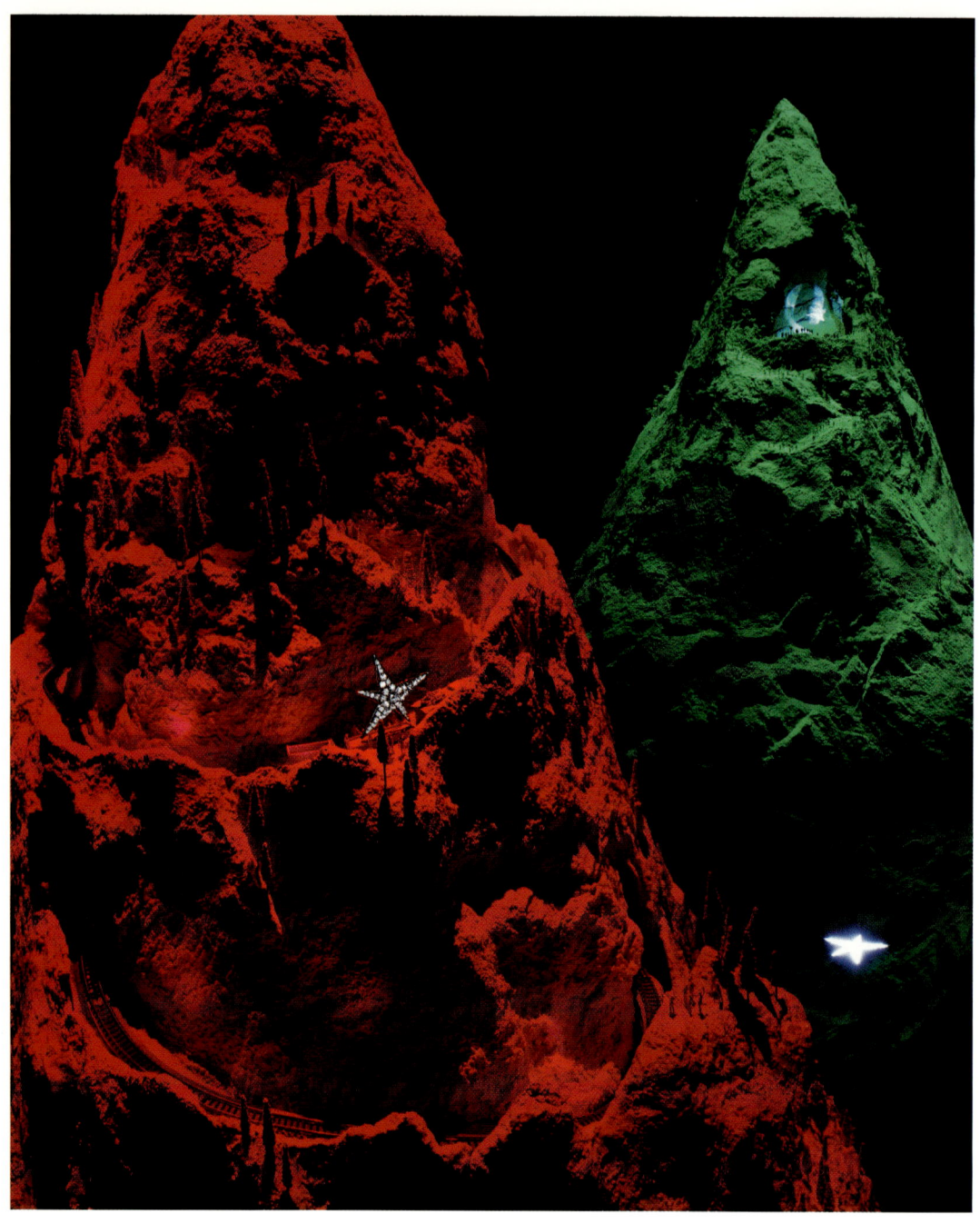

Top
Detail of the "Rêves de Diamants" exhibition, as imagined by Ingo Maurer.

Opposite
Variations in colour of the "Cosmos" watch in white gold and diamonds.

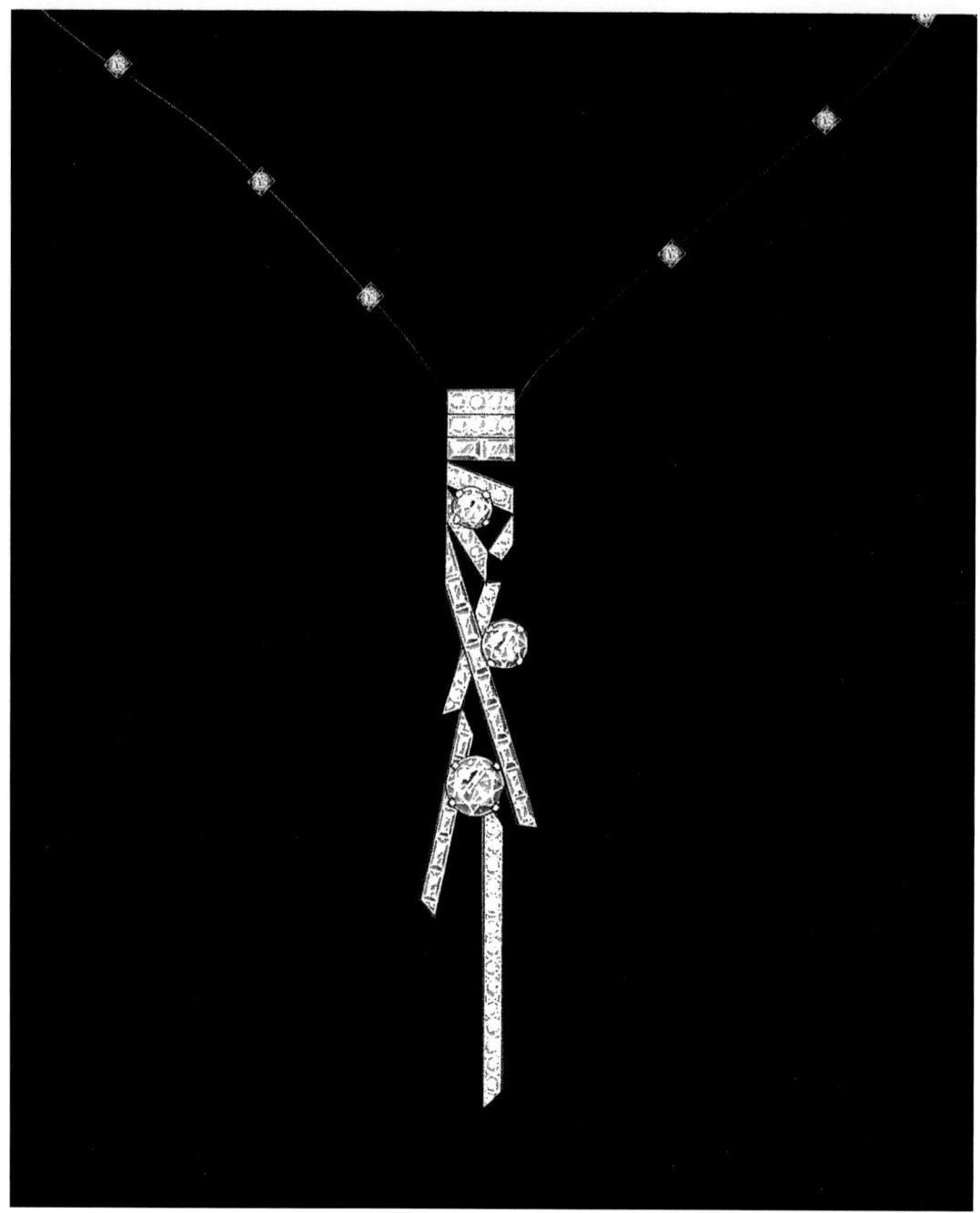

Top
Drawing of the "Givre" necklace in 18-karat white gold and diamonds.

Opposite
"Cosmos" watch in 18-karat white gold and diamonds on grosgrain bracelet.

Pages 122 and 123
"Haute Joaillerie" watch on grosgrain bracelet.

Top
Re-edition of the "Harmonie" ring in 18-karat white gold and diamonds, created by Mademoiselle Chanel in 1932.

Opposite
"Cosmos" watch in 18-karat white gold and 850 diamonds.

Top
"Cosmos" necklace in 18-karat white gold, diamonds and 5 rubies.

Opposite
"Bûche" watch in 18-karat white gold, diamonds and rubies.

Top
"Quilt ajouré" ring in 18-karat white gold and diamonds.

Opposite
"Bûche" watch in 18-karat white gold and diamonds.

Opposite
"Chocolat" watch in 18-karat white gold, entirely set with diamonds.

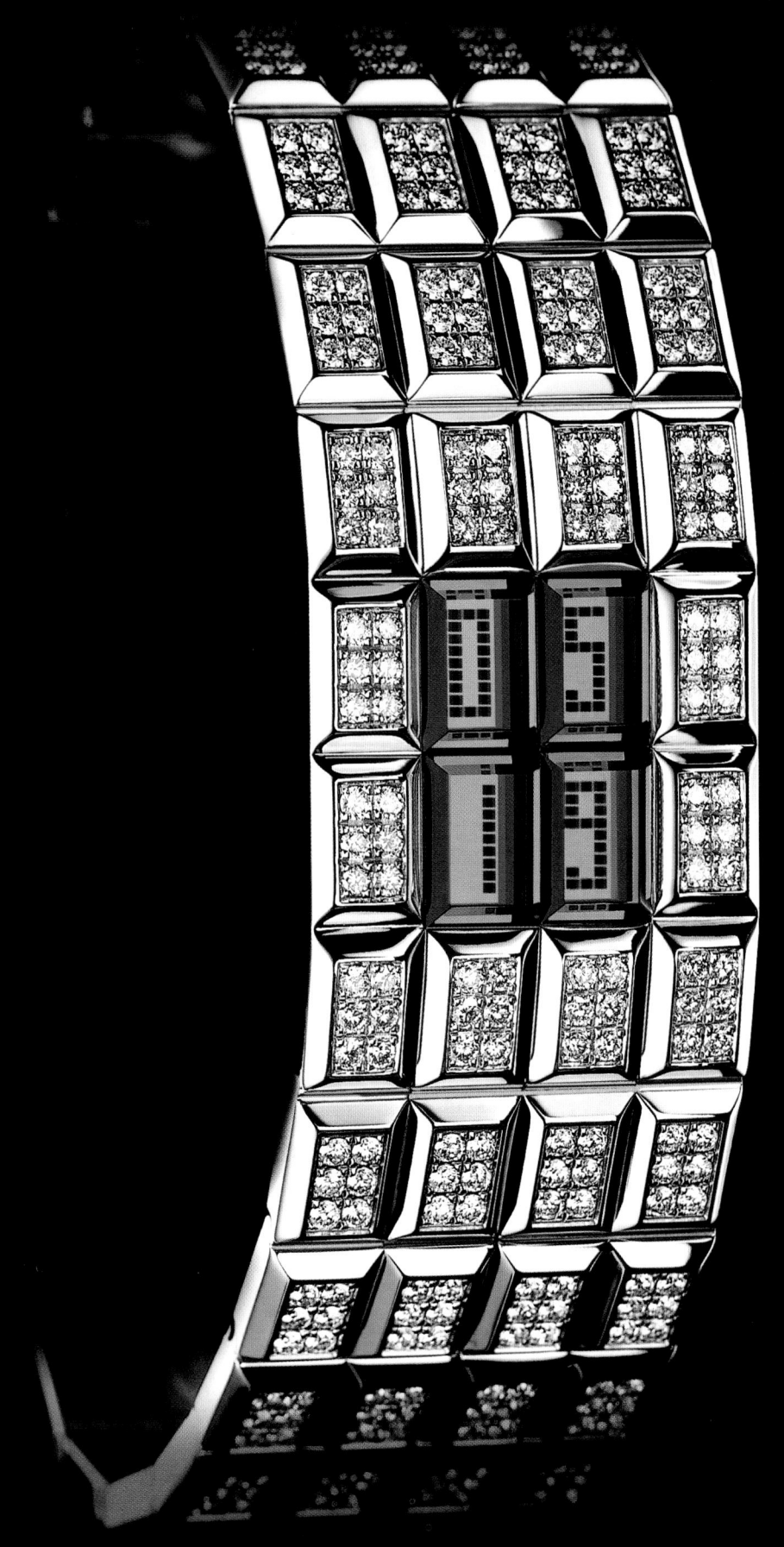

Top
Re-edition of the "Harmonie" bracelet in 18-karat white gold, onyx and diamonds, created by Mademoiselle Chanel in 1932.

Opposite
"Harmonie" watch in 18-karat white gold, onyx and diamonds.

Opposite
"Mademoiselle" watch in 18-karat white gold, set with diamonds.

Pages 136 and 137
Diamonds.

Opposite
"Première" watch in 18-karat yellow gold and diamonds, mother-of-pearl dial.

Top
"La Ronde" earrings in 18-karat white gold and diamonds.

Opposite
"La Ronde" watch in 18-karat white gold and diamonds on grosgrain bracelet.

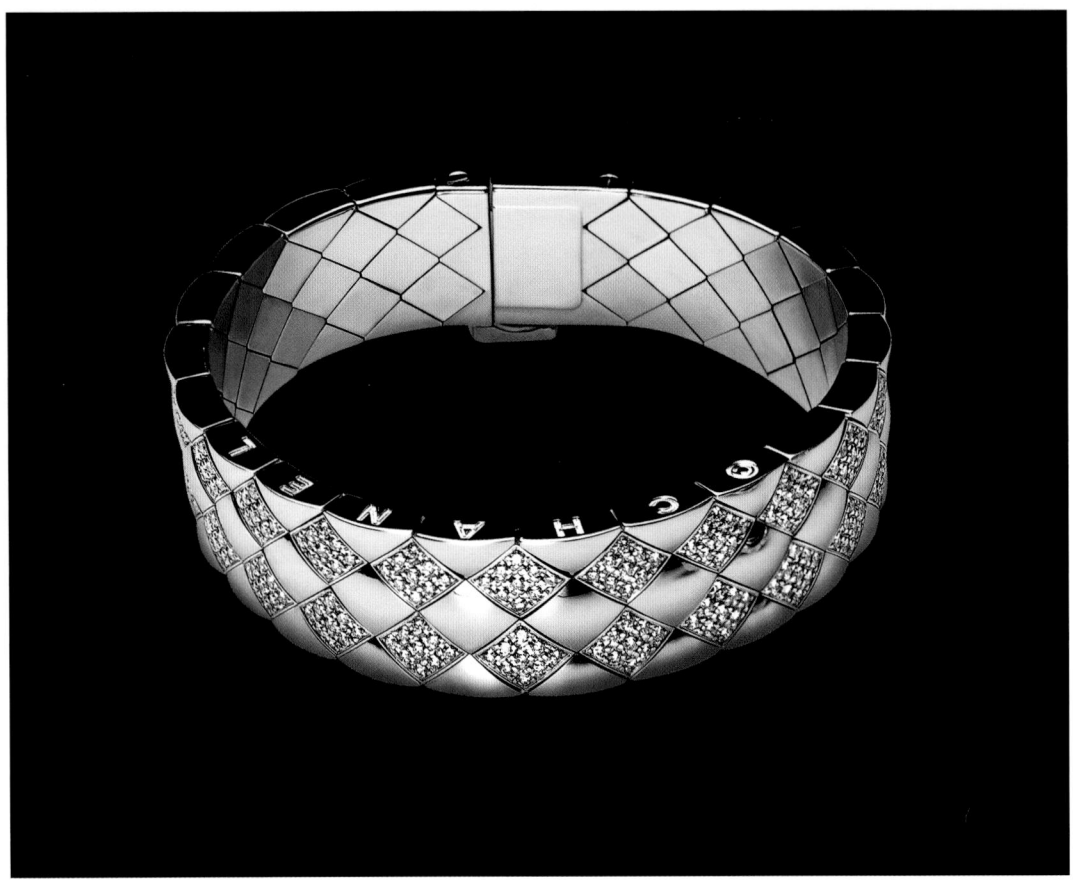

Top
"Matelassée Souple" bracelet in 18-karat white gold and diamonds.

Opposite
"Matelassée" watch in stainless steel and diamonds.

Top
White camellia, the symbol of Chanel.

Opposite
"Camélia Secret" watch in 18-karat white gold and diamonds, on grosgrain bracelet.

Opposite
"Camélia Secret" watch in 18-karat white gold and diamonds, on grosgrain bracelet.

COPYRIGHTS

6: Mademoiselle Chanel on the balcony of her apartment at the Ritz Hotel, in 1935 - R. Schall. **9**: Chanel Watch and Fine Jewellery Boutique, 18 Place Vendôme - Chanel. **11**: Jacques Helleu, Artistic Director of Chanel - Chanel. **12**: Drawing of a J12 by Jacques Helleu - Chanel. **16 ; 18 and 19**: Hand setting on a J12 dial ; Chanel watch-making workshops at La Chaux-de-Fonds in Switzerland - Chanel. **20**: Bezel polishing - Chanel. **21**: Dial setting - Chanel. **22 and 23**: Quality control - Chanel. **24**: Sapphire crystal glass setting - Chanel. **25**: Bracelet assembling - Chanel. **28 and 29**: Close-up of the J12 Chronograph dial - Chanel/Assouline. **30**: Source of inspiration - Groupe IMACOM. **31**: J12, water-resistant to 200 m - Chanel/Assouline. **32 and 33**: High-tech profile - Chanel/Assouline. **34**: Detail of an engine - Fotostudio Zumbrunn. **35**: Detail of the automatic J12 Chronograph movement, certified COSC (Official Swiss Chronometer Control) - Chanel/Assouline. **36 and 37 ; 38 and 39**: Black and White ; J12 in high-tech white ceramic, 38 mm - Chanel/Assouline. **40 and 41**: J12 bezel in high-tech ceramic and tungsten carbide - Chanel/Assouline. **42**: Bow of a black yacht - Elemond. **43**: Visual publicity of the J12, 38 mm - Chanel/Assouline. **44 and 45**: J12 in high-tech white ceramic, 38 mm - Chanel/Assouline. **46**: White sail - D.R. **47**: J12 in high-tech white ceramic and diamonds, 38 mm - Chanel/Assouline. **48 and 49**: Rain of diamonds on the J12 - Chanel/Assouline. **50 and 51 ; 52 and 53** : J12 white diamonds or black diamonds ; Positive/Negative of the J12 diamonds - Chanel/Assouline. **54**: J12, white diamonds - Chanel/Assouline. **55**: J12, black diamonds - Chanel/Assouline. **58 and 59**: Image from the "Matelassée" press kit in 1993 - Chanel/Assouline. **60**: "Matelassée" watch in stainless steel - Chanel. **61**: Detail of the stainless steel matelassé - Assouline. **62**: Detail of the two-tone matelassé - Assouline. **63**: "Matelassée" watch in 18-karat yellow gold - Chanel. **64**: "Matelassée Souple" ring in 18-karat yellow gold - Chanel. **65**: Bracelet flexibility of the "Matelassée" watch in 18-karat yellow gold - Chanel. **66 and 67**: Chanel matelassé to infinity - Assouline. **68**: "Ultra noir" necklace in 18-karat yellow gold and high-tech ceramic - Chanel. **69**: "Chocolat" watch in 18-karat yellow gold - Chanel. **71**: Drawing of the "Chocolat" watch in high-tech ceramic - Assouline. **72 and 73**: "Chocolat" watch in high-tech ceramic ; "Chocolat" watch in stainless steel - Chanel. **74 and 75**: The art of digital - Assouline. **76 and 77**: The famous N°5 ; "Chocolat" watch in 18-karat white gold, set with two rows of diamonds - Assouline. **78 and 79**: "Chocolat" watch in 18-karat yellow gold ; "Chocolat" watch in high-tech ceramic - Assouline. **80**: "Chocolat" watch in stainless steel - Assouline. **82**: Black geometry - Assouline. **83**: "Mademoiselle" watch in 18-karat white gold and baguette-cut diamonds - Chanel. **84**: "Mademoiselle" watch, white or black patent leather - Chanel. **85**: Picture from the press kit "Mademoiselle, White and Black" - Assouline. **86 and 87**: "Mademoiselle" watch, white dial on a satin finish stainless steel bracelet, or "Mademoiselle" watch, black dial on a mirror-polished, stainless steel bracelet - Chanel. **88**: Aerial view of the Place Vendôme - IGN. **89**: "Première" watch in stainless steel interwoven with leather - Chanel. **90**: Clasp detail of the platinum "Première" watch - Chanel/Assouline. **91**: Anecdote ! - D.R. **93**: Stainless steel chain bracelet "Première" watch, on Paul Morand's book *"L'Allure de Chanel"*, Karl Lagerfeld drawing. **94 and 95**: Stainless steel chain bracelet "Première" watch, mother-of-pearl dial - Chanel. **98**: "Lumière" necklace in 18-karat white gold, South Sea pearls and diamonds - Chanel. **99**: "Mademoiselle" watch in 18-karat yellow gold, cultured pearl bracelet - D.R. **100 and 101**: Mademoiselle Chanel by Cecil Beaton - Courtesy of Sotheby's London. **102**: "Matelassée Pearls" cuff bracelet in 18-karat yellow gold, cultured pearls and diamonds - Chanel. **103**: "Mademoiselle" watch in 18-karat yellow gold, cultured pearl bracelet - Chanel. **104**: Detail of the raw materials used in the "Camélia Secret" watch - Assouline. **105**: "Mademoiselle" watch in 18-karat yellow gold, cultured pearl bracelet - Chanel. **106**: "Camélia" brooch in 18-karat white gold, South Sea pearl and diamonds - Chanel. **107**: "Camélia Secret" watch in 18-karat white gold, cultured pearls and diamonds - Chanel. **108 and 109**: "Camélia Secret" watch in 18-karat white gold, cultured pearls, diamonds and rubies - Chanel. **112 and 113**: "Swing" necklace in 18-karat white gold, composed of 954 diamonds for a total weight of 39 carats and a central oval diamond of 7.50 carats - Chanel. **114**: Re-edition of the "Comète" necklace, created by Mademoiselle Chanel in 1932 - Chanel/Assouline. **115**: "Comète" watch in 18-karat white gold and diamonds on grosgrain bracelet - Chanel. **116**: Re-edition of the "Comète" brooch created by Mademoiselle Chanel in 1932 - Chanel. **117**: "Comète Secret" watch in 18-karat white gold and diamonds - Chanel. **118**: Detail of the "Rêves de Diamants" exhibition, as imagined by Ingo Maurer - Chanel/Assouline. **119**: Variations in colour of the "Cosmos" watch in white gold and diamonds - Chanel. **120**: Drawing of the "Givre" necklace in 18-karat white gold and diamonds - Chanel. **121**: "Cosmos" watch in 18-karat white gold and diamonds on grosgrain bracelet - Chanel. **122 and 123**: "Haute Joaillerie" watch on grosgrain bracelet - Chanel. **124**: Re-edition of the "Harmonie" ring in 18-karat white gold and diamonds, created by Mademoiselle Chanel in 1932 - Chanel. **125**: "Cosmos" watch in 18-karat white gold and 850 diamonds - Chanel. **126**: "Cosmos" necklace in 18-karat white gold, diamonds and 5 rubies - Chanel. **127**: "Bûche" watch in 18-karat white gold, diamonds and rubies - Chanel. **128**: "Quilt ajouré" ring in 18-karat white gold and diamonds - Chanel. **129**: "Bûche" watch in 18-karat white gold and diamonds - Chanel. **131**: "Chocolat" watch in 18-karat white gold, entirely set with diamonds - Chanel. **132**: Re-edition of the "Harmonie" bracelet in 18-karat white gold, onyx and diamonds, created by Mademoiselle Chanel in 1932 - Chanel. **133**: "Harmonie" watch in 18-karat white gold, onyx and diamonds - Chanel. **135**: "Mademoiselle" watch in 18-karat white gold, set with diamonds - Chanel. **136 and 137**: Diamonds - Assouline. **139**: "Première" watch in 18-karat yellow gold and diamonds, mother-of-pearl dial - Chanel. **140**: "La Ronde" earrings in 18-karat white gold and diamonds - Chanel/Assouline. **141**: "La Ronde" watch in 18-karat white gold and diamonds on grosgrain bracelet - Chanel/Assouline. **142**: "Matelassée Souple" bracelet in 18-karat white gold and diamonds - Chanel/Assouline. **143**: "Matelassée" watch in stainless steel and diamonds - Chanel. **144**: White camellia, the symbol of Chanel - Assouline. **145**: "Camélia Secret" watch in 18-karat white gold and diamonds, on grosgrain bracelet - Chanel. **147**: "Camélia Secret" watch in 18-karat white gold and diamonds, on grosgrain bracelet - Chanel.

Chanel 2003 (Société par actions simplifiées)
135, avenue Charles-de-Gaulle 92200 Neuilly-sur-Seine
RCS : 542 052 766 - Nanterre - Capital social : 10 000 000 euros
RÉF. : H1214 GB - 04/2003